Deidra's Dolly

To: William & Maeve
You are Perfect to Me!

♡
Linda S. Mai

OGHMA
CREATIVE MEDIA

Bentonville, Arkansas • Los Angeles, California
www.oghmacreative.com

Copyright © 2022 by Linda S. Mai
We are a strong supporter of copyright. Copyright represents creativity, diversity, and free speech, and provides the very foundation from which culture is built. We appreciate you buying the authorized edition of this book and for complying with applicable copyright laws by not reproducing, scanning, or distributing any part of it in any form without permission. Thank you for supporting our writers and allowing us to continue publishing their books.

Library of Congress Cataloging-in-Publication Data

Names: Mai, Linda S., author | Coble, Jain, illustrator
Title: Deidra's Dolly/Linda S. Mai |
Description: First Edition | Bentonville: Lee, 2022
Identifiers: LCCN: 2022943877 | ISBN: 978-1-63373-795-2 (hardcover) ISBN: 978-1-63373-794-5 (paperback) | ISBN: 978-1-63373-796-9 (eBook)
BISAC: JUVENILE FICTION/Health & Daily Living/Diseases, Illnesses & Injuries |
JUVENILE FICTION/ Social Themes/Emotions & Feelings | JUVENILE NONFICTION/Imagination & Play

LC record available at: https://lccn.loc.gov/2022943877

Lee Press paperback edition August, 2022

Cover & Interior Layout by Casey W. Cowan
Executive Editor: Chrissy Willis
Editor: Derek Hale & Amy Cowan

This book is a work of fiction. Any references to historical events, real people, or real places are used fictitiously. Other names, characters, places, and events are products of the author's imagination, and any resemblance to actual events or places or persons, living or dead, is entirely coincidental.

Published by Lee Press, an imprint of Young Dragons Press, a subsidiary of The Oghma Book Group.

Deidra's Dolly

Linda S. Mai
illustrated by Jain Coble

LEE PRESS

an imprint of
YOUNG DRAGONS PRESS

*To my parents, George and Ruth Williams,
who always said I could do anything if I worked at it.*

*And to my adoring cheering section:
my husband, siblings, kids, and grandkids.*

*Thank you to all my writing friends,
who mentored, critiqued, and supported
the creation of this book.*

Deidra frosted cookies with Dolly.
She played cards and climbed trees with Dolly.
But Deidra's favorite thing was
whispering secrets in Dolly's ear and
planning new adventures.

One day Deidra's new puppy chewed three fingers off Dolly's hand.

One weekend, Deidra's sneaky sister, Kayla, cut off a chunk of Dolly's hair. "I'm sorry this happened to you, but you're still perfect to me," Deidra said.

Then she danced Dolly around the room singing:

One night, Deidra's little brother, Oliver, decorated Dolly's legs with colored markers.

Then he tried to clean her off in the toilet.

"I'm sorry this happened to you, but you're still perfect to me," Deidra said. Then she dried her off with a fuzzy towel singing:

"Marker-Schmarker!
I don't care.

I found socks
we both can wear."

One morning Deidra had a high fever and was almost too weak to get out of bed.

Her mom and dad took her to see several doctors, who did lots of medical tests, but Deidra didn't get any better.

Deidra's grandparents came to stay with Kayla and Oliver.

Deidra boarded a plane with her parents and flew to a special hospital far away. In their rush to leave, Dolly was left behind.

At the hospital, the doctors did many, many more tests to find out what was wrong.

Deidra missed Dolly.

The nurses gave her lots and lots of medicine that made her feel yucky.

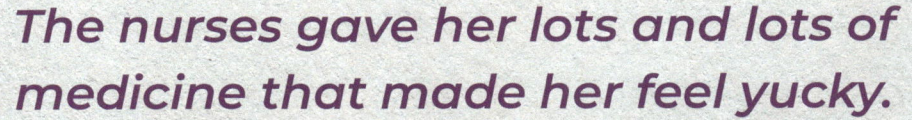

Deidra cried for Dolly.

... but he was terrible at cards and always fell over when she whispered in his ear.

Many weeks passed and slowly Deidra felt better. Sometimes she read Dolly's favorite book and pretended Dolly was sitting beside her.

She drew pictures of Dolly so she wouldn't forget her face.

When her doctor said she could leave the hospital, Deidra was anxious to get home. She wanted to see Kayla and Oliver, but couldn't wait to hug Dolly!

She rushed through the front door, scooped Dolly into her arms, snuggled her tight, and kissed her cheek.

"I missed you so much! Remember me?" Dolly didn't say anything, but in her heart, Deidra heard these words: "I'm sorry this happened to you, but you're still perfect to me."

"Baldy-Schmaldy! I don't care. I found hats we both can wear."

AUTHOR'S NOTE

Diedra's Dolly is a fictional story about a little girl who develops a life-threatening sickness. Cancer and other serious illnesses are a reality for many children and their families. Often, the medicine given to cancer patients causes side effects such as hair loss, loss of weight, fatigue, and weakness. This book is a reminder that even though we may look different, we are still the same inside and want to be loved. The author, herself a cancer survivor, has a soft heart for anyone—children as well as adults— battling this terrible disease.

For more information and resources on children stricken with cancer, please visit the following websites:

www.cancer.net/navigating-cancer-care/children/childhood-cancer-resources

www.acco.org/websites-for-kids-with-cancer

www.cancer.gov/types/childhood-cancers

www.cancer.org/cancer/cancer-in-children.html

The author hopes this book will reach the hearts of all children and parents who struggle through any illness, yet through it all, never allow the challenges they face to diminish their love for each other.

ABOUT THE CREATORS

about the author
LINDA S. MAI

Linda currently resides in Broken Arrow, Oklahoma with her husband, Chris. She has a master's degree in Elementary Education and taught third grade. Besides writing picture books and middle grade novels, she plays in a handbell choir, rides her ATV, and loves to travel, especially to see her children and grandchildren. Visit her at www.lindasmai.com.

about the illustrator
JAIN COBLE

Jain was born in a small ex-Soviet country called Moldova and moved to the USA at the age of ten. Growing up as an immigrant, she often felt that she could express herself through art when words weren't enough. She developed a strong appreciation for different cultures and diversity, which led her to study abroad and travel to over a dozen different countries (so far!). She feels most accomplished when her art sparks inspiration or a connection with the viewer and encourages you to reach out! Jain can be found on Instagram, Twitter, and Etsy, all under the same affirmation she claims proudly: JainMakesArt(.com)

CPSIA information can be obtained
at www.ICGtesting.com
Printed in the USA
BVHW020038100922
646702BV00002B/15